21 DAYS
IN CHRIST

LARRY STARKEY

NOBLE ROGUE
PUBLISHING

21 Days in Christ

Copyright © 2023 Larry Starkey

Unless otherwise noted, all Scripture quotations are from the ESV Bible (The Holy Bible, English Standard Version), copyright 2001 by Crossway, a publishing ministry of Good News Publishers. Used with permission. All rights reserved.

ISBN: 979-8-9893410-3-0

DEDICATION

This book is dedicated to my wife, Ethel. It's a joy to journey with you (for 35 years now and counting!) in discovering our blessings in Christ together.

TABLE OF CONTENTS

Introduction	1
Part 1: Your Salvation in Christ	**3**
Day 1: Salvation in Christ	5
Day 2: Grace in Christ	9
Day 3: Redemption in Christ	13
Day 4: Forgiveness in Christ	17
Day 5: Righteousness in Christ	21
Day 6: Reconciliation in Christ	25
Day 7: Chosen in Christ	29
Part 2: Your Security in Christ	**33**
Day 8: No Condemnation in Christ	35
Day 9: Free from the Law of Sin and Death in Christ	39
Day 10: Sealed with the Holy Spirit in Christ	43
Day 11: Spiritually Rooted and Built Up in Christ	47
Day 12: Eternal Life in Christ	51
Day 13: A Protected Heart and Mind in Christ	55
Day 14: Safe in God's Love in Christ	59
Part 3: Your Significance in Christ	**63**
Day 15: A Child of God in Christ	65
Day 16: A New Creation in Christ	69
Day 17: Created for Good Works in Christ	73
Day 18: Unified with Believers in Christ	77
Day 19: A New Walk in Christ	81
Day 20: Always Triumphant in Christ	85
Day 21: Hope in Christ	89
Notes	93
About the Author	95

"Blessed be the God and Father of our Lord Jesus Christ, who has blessed us in Christ with every spiritual blessing in the heavenly places."
(Ephesians 1:3)

INTRODUCTION

Readers may be surprised to learn that the two-word phrase "in Christ" is one of the most often used terms in the New Testament to describe a follower of Jesus Christ. In fact, "in Christ" (and its equivalent "in him," in the Lord," etc.) is used, remarkably, nearly 200 times in the New Testament!

"In Christ" is used so frequently because it accurately and fully describes God's view of the relationship a believer has with Christ that begins at salvation and continues throughout eternity. When we trust in Christ and His death and resurrection for salvation, God places us in a dynamic, eternal union with Christ—God now sees us as being "in Christ." And just as a small key can open a large door, the short phrase "in Christ" grants us access to all the blessings God has promised to believers. Ephesians 1:3 declares that God has "blessed us in Christ with every spiritual blessing." God's blessings reside in Christ. Thus, the blessed life is not found in a formula, an emotional experience, or in following rules; rather, it is found in a union with a Person: Jesus Christ. Everything Jesus *is* is all we'll ever need!

In this short book, I've chosen 21 of the blessings the New Testament says are ours in Christ, arranged them into the three categories below, and provided a basic explanation for each in a daily reading:

Salvation – In Christ, we are rescued from sin's consequences.
Security – In Christ, we are eternally secure.
Significance – In Christ, we find our identity and purpose.

With each daily reading is a short prayer of gratitude for the day's blessing in Christ, suggested verses for further Bible study, and three questions to prompt deeper thinking about the day's "in Christ" topic. My aim for these 21 devotional readings is to guide readers into a clearer understanding of and deeper appreciation for the spiritual blessings God has given us in Christ.

In Christ,
Larry Starkey
January, 2024

PART 1:
YOUR SALVATION IN CHRIST

DAY 1:
SALVATION IN CHRIST

> "I endure everything for the sake of the elect, that they also may obtain the salvation that is **in Christ** Jesus with eternal glory."
> (2 Timothy 2:10)

Roseann Sdoia was one of the 160 casualties wounded in the domestic terrorist strike on the 2013 Boston Marathon. After the two bombs exploded 12 seconds apart, Roseann lay on the ground dazed, burned, bloodied, deaf, and missing her right foot.

Mike Materia, a military veteran of Iraq and Boston firefighter, arrived in the smoke, gently loaded Roseann into an emergency vehicle, climbed in after her, held her burned hand all the way to the hospital....and never left Roseann's side.

A romance between Mike and Roseann bloomed amid the surgeries, doctor visits, and physical therapy sessions. Roseann was eventually released from the hospital in May 2013 where she learned to walk with a prosthetic leg that Mike helped her get.

Mike and Roseann went on their first date in June 2013, which led to Mike's proposal, and then to a small wedding later in 2013. Today, Mike and Roseann participate together in races and raising funds for physically challenged athletes.[1]

> Salvation is the act of God's love and grace by which He saves us from the consequences of sin and brings us into an eternal relationship with Himself.

We all love a rescue story, but when the rescue results in a romance and a relationship—the "rescued" marries the "rescuer"—it adds a sweet and special dimension to the story!

A rescue that leads to a relationship between the rescuer and the rescued serves as a beautiful and accurate picture of the Christian concept of salvation through Christ. This may seem unusual to many since salvation is often mistakenly associated with words like religion, rituals, and rules, not rescue or relationship! However, while the word "salvation" appears hundreds of times in Scripture and generally means "deliverance from danger," the New Testament crystalizes and clarifies it: Salvation is the act of God's love and grace by which He saves us from the consequences of sin (that's rescue!) and brings us into an eternal relationship with Himself (that's relationship!). Let's take a closer look at salvation in Christ as a rescue and relationship.

Sin has put us in danger. The Bible says that sin—our choice to rebel against God by going our own way instead of His way (1 Jn.3:4; Is.53:6)—has put us in danger. Our sin has separated us from God (Is.59:2), put us at enmity with Him (Rom.5:10), and will ultimately result in death and eternal separation from God in a terrible place of divine wrath called Hell (Rev.20:11-15).

We cannot save ourselves. No matter how hard we try to earn God's favor through good works or moral effort, we still fall short of God's perfect standard (Rom.3:20-23). There is nothing we can do to save ourselves—we are helpless and need rescued!

God rescues us through Jesus. God still loves us despite our sin (Rom.5:8). Since we cannot save ourselves, God came to us in Jesus Christ, the perfect God-Man, to provide forgiveness by taking our sin and its penalty to the cross and dying as our substitute (2 Cor.5:21; 1 Pet.2:24). Three days later, Jesus rose from the dead to verify that He had satisfied all of God's righteous demands and to give us new life and a right relationship with God (Rom.5:11). We experience this divine rescue by repenting toward God (acknowledging our personal sin against God) and placing our faith in Jesus alone (relying on Jesus and His finished work) (Acts 20:21).

Salvation includes a rescue from sin's consequences and a loving, eternal relationship with our Rescuer, Jesus. Jesus said in John 17:3, "This is eternal life, that they know you, the only true God, and Jesus Christ whom you have sent." The word know (v.3) indicates a deep knowledge gained through personal experience and intimate companionship with Christ.

A rescue that results in a relationship—that's what salvation is all about! And salvation is the starting point where all the other wonderful blessings God has promised us in Christ begin.

"In Christ" Prayer of Gratitude:
Thank You, Lord, for salvation where all Your wonderful blessings "in Christ" begin.

For Further Bible Study: What key words and phrases about salvation stand out to you in Philippians 3:3-11?

Questions to Dig Deeper

1. What is a key truth God taught me about Himself and His character through today's devotional?
   _____
   _____
   _____
   _____
   _____
   _____
   _____
   _____

2. What is a key truth God taught me about myself and who I am through today's devotional?
   _____
   _____
   _____
   _____
   _____
   _____
   _____
   _____

3. What step does God want me to take in response to what He taught me in today's devotional?
   _____
   _____
   _____
   _____
   _____
   _____
   _____
   _____

DAY 2:
GRACE IN CHRIST

> "You then, my child, be strengthened by the grace that is **in Christ** Jesus."
> (2 Timothy 2:1)

In his book *How You Can Be Sure You Will Spend Eternity with God*, Erwin Lutzer tells about a friendship between a missionary in India and a Hindu pearl diver. Although the two men had discussed salvation on many occasions, the Hindu could not accept the idea it was so costly that Jesus had to buy it for us with His death on the cross, and we can only receive it as a gift from God. The Hindu believed salvation had to be earned by walking on his knees for nine hundred miles to Delhi.

As he was leaving on his pilgrimage, the Hindu gave the missionary the largest, most perfect pearl he'd ever seen. The pearl, the Hindu explained, was found by his own beloved son who died while retrieving it from the bottom of the sea. Thanking him, the missionary then insisted on paying for the pearl. The Hindu was offended, declaring that the pearl cost him the life of his dear son—there was no price the missionary could pay for it.

At that moment, the truth about grace became clear to the Hindu: God's gift of salvation cost Him the life of His beloved Son—there's no price anyone could pay for it. To think we can somehow pay for or earn salvation is an insult to God, indeed. Lutzer concludes, "Grace is free to us but very costly to God."[2]

> Grace is the unmerited favor God extends to unworthy sinners who are deserving of punishment.

One of the clearest teachings in the Bible regarding the salvation we have in Christ is that it comes by God's grace through faith in Christ—there is nothing we can do to purchase, earn, or deserve it. Grace is the unmerited favor God extends to unworthy sinners who are deserving of punishment.

One of the greatest verses in the Bible about grace is Ephesians 2:8: "For by grace you have been saved through faith. And this is not your own doing; it is the gift of God." Let's take a closer look at the five key phrases that make up this verse:

"For by grace" (v.8a) – Grace is God's part of salvation. God was under no obligation to provide salvation for us. Salvation is all God's idea—it is only by His loving initiative and gracious favor that we can be saved.

"you have been saved" (v.8b) – As we learned in our Day 1 reading, salvation is the act of God's love and grace by which He saves us from the consequences of sin and brings us into an eternal relationship with Himself. This is why the Bible refers to people who have experienced salvation as being "saved" (Acts 16:31; Rom.10:9-10; 10:13, etc.). Being saved implies that we were in danger, helpless to save ourselves, and needed rescued. Grace is the basis upon which "Christ Jesus came into the world to save sinners" (1 Tim.1:15).

"through faith" (v.8c) – Faith is our part of salvation. It involves our heart, mind, and will. God offers salvation, then we respond by believing in our heart that we need saved, understanding with our mind that salvation is offered in Christ, and deciding with our will to receive salvation by trusting in Christ and His death and resurrection.

"And this is not your own doing" (v.8d) – The teachings of every religion in the world regarding salvation can be summarized in only two words: 1) Do: You must do something to earn or pay for salvation—this is the teaching of every non-Christian religion, or 2) Done: God has already done through Christ all that is necessary for salvation—Christianity alone teaches this. The Bible is clear that salvation comes by God's grace through our faith in what Christ has finished for us through His death and resurrection.

"it is the gift of God" (v.8e) – Salvation comes by receiving God's gift, not by giving something to God; by trusting in Christ, not by trying to do or pay something. Romans 11:6 declares, "If it is by grace, it is no longer on the basis of works; otherwise, grace would no longer be grace."

"In Christ" Prayer of Gratitude:
God, I thank You for grace in Christ—Your unmerited favor which was free to me but very costly to You.

For Further Bible Study: How do these verses highlight God's grace: Romans 3:24, 2 Corinthians 8:9, James 4:6?

Questions to Dig Deeper

1. What is a key truth God taught me about Himself and His character through today's devotional?

   _____
   _____
   _____
   _____
   _____
   _____
   _____

2. What is a key truth God taught me about myself and who I am through today's devotional?

   _____
   _____
   _____
   _____
   _____
   _____
   _____

3. What step does God want me to take in response to what He taught me in today's devotional?

   _____
   _____
   _____
   _____
   _____
   _____
   _____

DAY 3: REDEMPTION IN CHRIST

"**In him** we have redemption through his blood…"
(Ephesians 1:7a)

Thousands of people a year visit the Christ Church Cathedral—a magnificent edifice built in 1873 in Stone Town, Zanzibar, Tanzania. The reason so many people are attracted to the church is because it was built on Mkunazini Road in the center of town where the largest slave market in East Africa once was. The church's altar is said to be in the precise spot where the main whipping post of the market was located. Inside the church is a cross made from the wood of the tree that grows on the place where the heart of Christian missionary to Africa and slavery abolitionist David Livingstone was buried.

The Christian leaders who envisioned the cathedral's construction wanted it to be a visible declaration that the center of town would no more be a place of evil and enslavement. The Christ Church Cathedral is a beautiful, powerful symbol of the freedom all believers in Christ find from the chains and enslavement of sin.

> Redemption is the act by which God purchased our freedom from enslavement to sin and liberated us to serve Him.

The word "redemption" means "to purchase and set free by paying a price." In the ancient world's slave markets, when a price was paid for a slave, he was released to go live with and serve his new owner. Through the cross of Christ, God redeemed us—that is, He purchased our freedom from enslavement and liberated us to fellowship with and serve Him.

Our redemption price was paid by "[Christ'] blood" (Eph.1:7). When the Bible refers to the blood of Christ, it is referring to Jesus' death in all its saving aspects. To shed or remove blood means to end life. Since "the wages of sin is death" (Rom.6:23), the shedding of blood—or death—was God's way of effecting salvation.

In the Old Testament, once a year the high priest drained the blood of animals and sprinkled it on the mercy seat in the Holy of Holies, symbolically covering the people's sins. However, the high priest would have to repeat this action year after year—the blood of the animal sacrifices could only cover the people's sins temporarily; animal blood could not remove sin's guilt permanently (Heb.10:11). But the New Testament declares that the blood of Christ cleanses (not just covers) our sin permanently (not just temporarily). Jesus "entered once for all into the holy places, not by means of the blood of goats and calves but by means of his own blood, thus securing an eternal redemption" (Heb.9:12). Thanks to Jesus, "the lamb of God who takes away the sins of the world" (Jn.1:29), and His shed blood which "cleanses us from all sin" (1 Jn.1:7), our sins are gone forever, never to be brought to God's attention again.

Christ redeems us from the guilt associated with sin. Guilt is not just a feeling; it is the cursed and condemned condition a sinner is in before God due to breaking His law. But Galatians 3:13 states, "Christ redeemed us from the curse of the law." Christ's payment through His death on the cross forever absolves believers from all the guilt, blame, and curse associated with sin.

Christ redeems us from sin's slavery so we can live for God. Titus 2:14 says, "[Christ] gave himself for us to redeem us from all lawlessness and to purify for himself a people for his own possession who are zealous for good works." Although sin is not completely eradicated from our lives after salvation, nor is the desire to sin fully removed, sin's dominion over us has been broken. The desire to sin remains, but the obligation to sin is gone. We are now free—not free to sin, but free not to sin.

Christ has liberated us from sin the slave owner—now we are free to serve God. Christ will redeem us from bondage to our bodies of sin. Romans 8:23 says, "We groan inwardly as we wait eagerly for…the redemption of our bodies." Today, our physical bodies are subject to disease, suffering, and death. But when Jesus returns, He "will transform our lowly body to be like his glorious body" (Php.3:21). Every pain and frailty related to our earthly body will be traded for a new, glorified body made fit to live forever with Christ!

"In Christ" Prayer of Gratitude:
Lord, thank You that in Christ I have been liberated from sin the slave owner, and I am now free to serve God.

For Further Bible Study: What other blessings are attributed to the blood of Christ (His death) in Romans 3:25 and Colossians 1:20?

Questions to Dig Deeper

1. What is a key truth God taught me about Himself and His character through today's devotional?

   _____
   _____
   _____
   _____
   _____
   _____
   _____
   _____

2. What is a key truth God taught me about myself and who I am through today's devotional?

   _____
   _____
   _____
   _____
   _____
   _____
   _____
   _____

3. What step does God want me to take in response to what He taught me in today's devotional?

   _____
   _____
   _____
   _____
   _____
   _____
   _____
   _____

DAY 4:
FORGIVENESS IN CHRIST

"**In him** we have...the forgiveness of our trespasses..."
(Ephesians 1:7b)

In his book, *Key Words of the Christian Life*, Warren Wiersbe tells the story of a man in England who put his Rolls Royce on a ferryboat and went across the English Channel to the Continent on a vacation. "While he was driving around Europe, something happened to the motor of his car. He cabled the Rolls Royce people back in England and asked, 'I'm having trouble with my car; what do you suggest I do?' Well, the Rolls-Royce people flew a mechanic over! The mechanic repaired the car and flew back to England, leaving the man to continue his holiday. As you can imagine, the fellow was wondering, How much is this going to cost me? So, when he got back to England, he wrote a letter and asked how much he owed them. He received a letter from the office that read, 'Dear Sir: There is no record anywhere in our files that anything ever went wrong with a Rolls Royce.'"

> Forgiveness is the act of God by which He dismisses our sins and no longer takes them into account based upon Christ's finished work on the cross.

Wiersbe continues: "The devil accuses you, you accuse yourself, maybe your friends accuse you; but God checks the file and says, 'There is no record anywhere in this file that My child ever did anything wrong.'"[3]

The word "forgiveness" (Eph.1:7) means "dismissed." It refers to the action an Old Testament high priest would take on the Day of Atonement when he would symbolically transfer all the sins of the Israelites to a goat, then release the goat into the wilderness, picturing their sins being dismissed or carried away (Leviticus 16). (This is where we get the term "scapegoat.")

Based upon Christ's finished work on the cross, God forgives our sins—that is, He dismisses them and no longer takes them into account. Our forgiveness in Christ means that there is no record anywhere in our file that we ever did anything wrong!

Note some other biblical action words that describe forgiveness:

God casts our sins into the depths of the sea. Micah 7:19 says, "You will cast all our sins into the depths of the sea." Through the cross of Christ, our sin has been symbolically jettisoned into the deepest sea, sinking like a rock toward an endless bottom, making our sin forever lost and irretrievable. Corrie ten Boom said, "God takes our sins—the past, present, and future—and dumps them into the sea and puts up a sign that says, 'No Fishing Allowed.'"

God removes our sin as far as the east is from the west. Psalm 103:12 says, "As far as the east is from the west, so far does he remove our transgressions from us." The directions of north and south are finite—they meet at the North and South Poles. But East and West are infinite—they have no Poles; they extend endlessly in opposite directions, and thus they never meet. God forgives us by removing our sin "as far as the east is from the west" (v.12)—He sends our sin as far away as we can possibly imagine, and they will never come back to condemn us!

God tosses our sins behind His back. Isaiah 38:17 says, metaphorically, that God puts our sins behind His back so He cannot see them anymore: "You have cast all my sins behind your back." Once God tosses our sins over His shoulder, He says, "Good riddance!" and never turns to look at our sins again—He has totally separated Himself from our sin!

God lifts the burden of sin from us. In Psalm 32:5, David writes, "You forgave the iniquity of my sin." The Hebrew word translated "forgave" means "to lift." When God forgave David, He lifted sin and its penalty off David forever. This reminds us of Pilgrim's Progress when Christian's heavy burden, symbolizing his sin, guilt, and dread of God's judgment, slides off his shoulders upon his arrival at Deliverance (the Cross), and he is never weighed down by guilt again. In Christ, we need never to be burdened by guilt again.

"In Christ" Prayer of Gratitude:
Thank You, Lord, that in Christ my sins are forgiven—dismissed forever—and will never be held against me.

For Further Bible Study: What other action words do you see in these verses that describe God's forgiveness of our sins: Psalm 32:1-2; 51:1-2, and Colossians 2:14?

Questions to Dig Deeper

1. What is a key truth God taught me about Himself and His character through today's devotional?

   _____
   _____
   _____
   _____
   _____
   _____
   _____

2. What is a key truth God taught me about myself and who I am through today's devotional?

   _____
   _____
   _____
   _____
   _____
   _____
   _____

3. What step does God want me to take in response to what He taught me in today's devotional?

   _____
   _____
   _____
   _____
   _____
   _____
   _____

DAY 5:
RIGHTEOUSNESS IN CHRIST

> "For our sake he made him to be sin who knew no sin, so that **in him** we might become the righteousness of God."
> (2 Corinthians 5:21)

Imagine two books: One is entitled *The Life of Christ* and contains a comprehensive, detailed record of Jesus' sinless, righteous life. What a beautiful book! The other book is called *The Life of (Your Name)* and contains a comprehensive, detailed record of all your sins and selfish actions. What an awful book!

Now imagine Jesus switching the covers of the books. He places the cover of your awful book over the contents of His own wonderful book. Now when you read *The Life of (Your Name)*, you see no sins or selfish actions listed—all you see is the record of Jesus' sinless, righteous life! The new book is so precious that God keeps it forever. The righteousness of Christ has been fully credited to you who were hopelessly unrighteous![4]

At the cross, God not only forgave and removed our sin, but He also added, or credited, Christ's righteousness to our account! The theological word for this action is "imputation." Wrapped up in the term imputation is the three-steps that ultimately led to God's crediting Christ's righteousness to the believer.

> Imputation is the act of God by which He credits Christ's righteousness to the believer's account.

First, Adam's sin and guilt were imputed (credited) to every human being, ruining our standing with God and subjecting us to God's judgment. Romans 5:12 says, "Sin came into the world through one man, and death through sin, and so death spread to all men because all sinned." Notice sin's tragic progression that began with Adam. First, sin entered the world through Adam's sin (v.12a), then death followed sin (v.12b), then death was passed down like an inheritance to all of Adam's descendants, which includes you, me, and all other human beings (v.12c).

David understood about the sin nature that had been passed down to him from Adam, and he grieved: "I was brought forth in iniquity, and in sin did my mother conceive me" (Psalm 51:5). Romans 5:18-19 says, "One trespass led to condemnation for all men…by the one man's disobedience the many were made sinners." No matter how morally upright we may try to live, God still counts us guilty because of Adam's sin being imputed to us. No wonder Jesus told Nicodemus that he must be "born again" (Jn. 3:7).

Second, our sins and guilt were imputed (credited) to Christ on the cross. 2 Corinthians 5:21a says, "For our sake he made him to be sin who knew no sin…" On the cross, Jesus became sin for us, answering for the guilt of our sin and absorbing God's judgment for us. The sinless became sin for the sinful. This was typified in the Old Testament when the sins of the person offering a sacrifice were transferred to the sacrificial animal that paid for the sins with its death.

This "transferal" of sin from the guilty to guiltless pictured what Christ, the "lamb without blemish or spot" (1 Pet.1:19) would accomplish for us as "the Lamb of God who takes away the sins of the world" (Jn.1:29).

The imputation of sin from the guilty to the guiltless was also prophesied in the Old Testament by Isaiah: "the Lord has laid on him the iniquity of us all" (Is.53:6). God charged our sins to Christ's account, and He made our payment for us even when we were estranged from Him. Romans 5:8 says, "God shows his love for us in that while we were still sinners, Christ died for us."

Third, Christ's righteousness is imputed (credited) to us at salvation. 2 Corinthians 5:21b says, "…so that in him we might become the righteousness of God." When God looks at a believer, He does not see sin; instead, He sees Christ's righteousness that has been credited to the believer. Our sin debt has been canceled, and Christ's righteousness has been deposited into our account. God considers Christ's righteousness to be ours. In Christ, God not only cancels our sins, but He also counts us as righteous! Romans 4:6 assures us of the "blessing of the one to whom God counts righteousness apart from works."

"In Christ" Prayer of Gratitude:
Lord, thank You that although I am a sinner by birth and by choice, you pardoned my sin and declared me righteous in Christ.

For Further Bible Study: How does Philippians 3:8-9 highlight the importance of imputation of the righteousness of Christ to believers?

Questions to Dig Deeper

1. What is a key truth God taught me about Himself and His character through today's devotional?

2. What is a key truth God taught me about myself and who I am through today's devotional?

3. What step does God want me to take in response to what He taught me in today's devotional?

DAY 6:
RECONCILIATION IN CHRIST

"**In Christ** God was reconciling the world to himself, not counting their trespasses against them."
(2 Corinthians 5:19)

American author Earnest Hemingway was awarded the Nobel Prize in Literature in 1954. He published seven novels, six short-story collections, and two nonfiction books. One of Hemmingway's lesser-known short stories, less than twenty pages long, is called *The Capital of the World*.

The story revolves around a young man named Paco who left home to follow his dream of becoming a bullfighter in Madrid, Spain. To emphasize how popular the name Paco (short for Francisco) is, Hemingway tells of a Spanish legend about a father who, after searching unsuccessfully all over Madrid for his estranged son, placed an ad in the daily Madrid newspaper: "Paco, Meet me at Hotel Montana Noon Tuesday. All is forgiven. Papa" all in hopes that the boy would see the ad and come to the Hotel Montana where they could be reconciled.

On Tuesday at noon, the father arrived at the hotel and could not believe what he saw. An entire squadron of police officers had been called out to keep order among hundreds of young men—each was named Paco, and each had read the ad and come to meet his respective father in front of the Hotel Montana to find the forgiveness each desperately needed.

> Reconciliation is the act of God by which He restores rebellious sinners into a favorable relationship with Himself.

Hemingway may have been making light of the number of young men named Paco living in Madrid, but he touched upon a universal truth: All of us are estranged from God, the heavenly Father, and have a longing deep down (whether we acknowledge it or not) to be forgiven and restored to Him. The Bible says that our sin put us at enmity with God in a state of self-declared war against Him (Rom.5:10a) and deserving His wrath (Rom.1:18). But "in Christ God was reconciling the world to himself, not counting their trespasses against them" (2 Cor.5:19). The word "reconcile" refers to God's work through Christ by which He restores believers to a favorable relationship with Himself "by the death of his Son" (Rom.5:10b). Now, in Christ, we have "peace with God" (Rom.5:1) and can face Him without shame or guilt.

God's reconciling love is powerfully illustrated in Jesus' parable of the prodigal son which unfolds in three stages:

Rebellion (Lk.15:11-16) – A rebellious young man demands that his father give him his inheritance, then runs away from home and wastes the money in sinful living. The son's desire for independence from his father represents our desire for independence from God's authority. At its core, sin is when we choose our own will and way instead of God's will and way (Is.53:6).

Repentance (Lk.15:17-20a) – The son runs into trouble and comes to his senses about his lost condition and his rebellious choices which led there. Longing to be right with his father, he decides to go back home, admit his mistake in leaving, and ask his father to take him in as a servant. Humbly admitting the fact of our own sin is an essential aspect of our being reconciled to God.

Reconciliation (Lk.15:20b-24) – The father notices his son afar off, runs to him, embraces him, kisses him, gladly forgives him, and orders a celebration. The father's reaction expresses how our heavenly Father feels towards sinners who repent: He longs to embrace us and reconcile us back to Himself!

It is well-known that later in his life, Ernest Hemingway, consumed with depression, anxiety, and loneliness, killed himself with a shotgun. What is not as well known is that Hemingway had grown up in a Christian home in Oak Park, Illinois where he heard the gospel many times. His grandparents were missionaries, and his father was a committed church member. What a tragedy that Hemingway, as far as we know, never experienced peace with God. Let's thank God for His reconciling invitation: "(Your name) meet Me at the cross today. All is forgiven. Your heavenly Father."

"In Christ" Prayer of Gratitude:
Thank You, Lord, for forgiving my sin and reconciling me back to Yourself in Christ.

For Further Bible Study: How do Romans 5:5 and Colossians 1:20 emphasize our reconciliation to God?

Questions to Dig Deeper

1. What is a key truth God taught me about Himself and His character through today's devotional?

   _____
   _____
   _____
   _____
   _____
   _____
   _____
   _____

2. What is a key truth God taught me about myself and who I am through today's devotional?

   _____
   _____
   _____
   _____
   _____
   _____
   _____
   _____

3. What step does God want me to take in response to what He taught me in today's devotional?

   _____
   _____
   _____
   _____
   _____
   _____
   _____
   _____

DAY 7: CHOSEN IN CHRIST

"[God] chose us **in him** before the foundation of the world, that we should be holy and blameless before him."
(Ephesians 1:4)

In his book *A Forgiving God in an Unforgiving World*, Ron Lee Davis tells a story about being chosen by grace. On his walk to school, a boy stopped by a pet store to watch through the window four puppies playing together.

When he got home, he pled with his mother to let him have one of the puppies. He even pledged to work extra chores around the house to earn money to help pay for the puppy. After thinking about it for a while, the mom consented, saying, "You can have the puppy, but I'll expect you to take care of it." The boy assured her: "I will, Mom."

The boy excitedly went to the pet store to buy his new puppy. After determining that the boy had enough money, the manager of the pet shop brought him to the window to select his puppy. After a few moments, the boy declared, "I'll take the little one in the corner." The shop owner said, "I don't recommend that one. Something is wrong with one of his legs—see how he just sits there. He can't run and play like the other dogs. Pick a different one."

> God chose us in Christ even though He was not obligated to do so and we were undeserving.

Without saying a word, the boy reached down and lifted his pant leg, revealing to the manager a chrome leg brace. "No," the boy firmly replied, "I'll take the puppy in the corner."[5]

What disqualified the puppy from being chosen by others was exactly what qualified him to be chosen by the boy.

Many of us say we believe in God's love and grace but think God's love and grace only applies to us when we are perfect—no blemishes, imperfections, disabilities, or scars. But the Bible tells us that the very brokenness that we thought disqualified us is exactly what qualifies us to be chosen by God in His love and grace. Our value and significance are found in realizing that God chose us in love because we acknowledge we are broken and need Him the most!

God chose us when He didn't have to. Ephesians 1:4 begins by informing us that God "chose us in him." A choice indicates that a decision was made to select one thing when faced with two or more possibilities. God was under no obligation to choose us. In fact, He knew that we would sin and turn against Him—He had every right to choose to reject and condemn us. Yet, He chose to love and extend grace to us anyway! Romans 5:8 says, "God shows his love for us in that while we were still sinners, Christ died for us."

God chose us before the world was even created. Ephesians 1:4 continues by informing us that God chose us "before the foundation of the world." Before anything was ever created, God knew each of us, loved us, prepared to offer Himself as a sacrifice to save us from our sin, and to invite us to Himself. In fact, this is one of the reasons God created the world and all that is in it in the first place—to give us a place to live, to thrive, and to fellowship with Him. God chose us, then created everything for His glory and for us: "that all the peoples of the earth may know that the Lord is God; there is no other" (1 Kings 8:60).

God chose us so that we would be set apart from nonbelievers and our old way of living, and faultless when our enemy accuses us. Ephesians 1:4 concludes: "that we should be holy and blameless before him." The word "holy" means set apart—that is, in God's eyes, we are removed from those who reject God and from our old way of living that left God out, and we are set unto Him who is holy. The word "blameless" means that God's sees us as without blame in Christ. Because we have become "the righteousness of God in [Christ]" (2 Cor.5:21), no charges by Satan, "the accuser" (Rev.12:10) can stick to us.

God chose us to tell everyone about Him. 1 Peter 2:9 says, "You are a chosen race...that you may proclaim the excellencies of him." God chose us and saved us so we would speak of His qualities, distinctions, and perfections to the world!

"In Christ" Prayer of Gratitude:
Thank You, God, for choosing me in Christ.

For Further Bible Study: What excellencies of God are mentioned in Acts 7:2, 55, Romans 15:5, 13, 2 Corinthians 1:3-4, and Philippians 4:9?

Questions to Dig Deeper

1. What is a key truth God taught me about Himself and His character through today's devotional?

2. What is a key truth God taught me about myself and who I am through today's devotional?

3. What step does God want me to take in response to what He taught me in today's devotional?

PART 2:
YOUR SECURITY IN CHRIST

DAY 8:
NO CONDEMNATION IN CHRIST

"There is therefore now no condemnation
for those who are **in Christ** Jesus."
(Romans 8:1)

There is a clause in the Fifth Amendment to the U.S. Constitution called the "Double Jeopardy Clause." It guarantees a person that once they have been tried for a crime, they cannot be tried for that same crime again—they cannot be prosecuted twice for the same crime: "No person shall…be subject for the same offense to be twice put in jeopardy of life or limb…"[6]

In a sense, we could say that our eternal security in Christ is based upon "God's Law of Double Jeopardy." Jesus Christ took our place on the cross and was fully prosecuted for our sins—and once is all that God's law demands. 1 Peter 3:18 says, "Christ…suffered once for sins, the righteous for the unrighteous, that he might bring us to God." Through His substitutionary death, Christ satisfied the payment due for our sin. If God were to put a believer's sins on Jesus and then also on the believer, that would be double jeopardy. We who have trusted in Christ's sacrifice have been acquitted and are exempt from eternal punishment for our sins, not because of a constitutional legal clause, but because of God's justice, love, and grace. Romans 8:1 assures the person who is in Christ: "There is therefore now no condemnation for those who are in Christ Jesus." Jesus said, "I give them eternal life, and they will never perish, and no one will snatch them out of my hand" (Jn.10:28). God has given us three sources of assurance that once we are saved, we are eternally secure in Christ.

> Once a believer is saved, he is eternally secure in Christ and is in no danger of ever losing his salvation.

The work of Christ justifies us forever. Romans 3:24 says, "We are justified by his grace as a gift, through the redemption that is in Christ Jesus." Justification is the judicial act by which God declares righteous those who believe in Jesus Christ. When we trust in Christ, we are justified, and God will never reverse His word of acquittal! Romans 5:1 assures us: "Since we have been justified by faith, we have peace with God through our Lord Jesus Christ."

The Word of God guarantees our salvation. 1 John 5:13 says, "I write these things to you who believe in the name of the Son of God that you may know that you have eternal life." One reason why God gave us the Bible and preserved it throughout the centuries is so we'd have something upon which to rest our faith that we are eternally secure. Our assurance of salvation does not rest upon the shaky ground of our feelings or the ups and downs of our spiritual progress; rather, the foundation of our assurance is God's eternal Word! Since God's Word will never pass away (Mk.13:31), then God's promise of our eternal security will never pass away!

The witness of the Spirit assures us that we are saved. Romans 8:16 says, "The Spirit himself bears witness with our spirit that we are children of God." The Holy Spirit, who resides in a believer's life from the moment of salvation (Eph.1:13), continually assures us in the depths of our hearts that we are God's children.

But what about a person who claims to be a Christian, yet lives an unrepentant lifestyle in sin with no interest in obeying God's Word? Or a person who claims to be a Christian but later leaves the faith? Do they lose their salvation? We cannot judge a person's heart (only God can), but we can inspect a person's fruit, or outward evidence of their claims: "You will recognize them by their fruits" (Mat.7:16). While all believers struggle with sin (Rom.7:13-25), a person who truly follows Christ will, over time, show a humble, ongoing awareness of and grief over their sin, and some measurable degree of growth in holiness and the fruit of the Spirit (Gal.5:22-23). A person who lives at peace with known sin shows that they likely never experienced salvation to begin with, not that they had salvation and then lost it. Similarly, a person who claims to be a Christian but later leaves the faith did not have salvation and then lose it; rather, their apostasy reveals they never had salvation to begin with. 1 John 2:19 says: "They went out from us, but they were not of us; for if they had been of us, they would have continued with us. But they went out, that it might become plain that they all are not of us."

"In Christ" Prayer of Gratitude:
God, thank You for saving me and keeping me
eternally secure in Christ.

For Further Bible Study: How is eternal security emphasized in Ephesians 4:30 and Jude 24?

Questions to Dig Deeper

1. What is a key truth God taught me about Himself and His character through today's devotional?

2. What is a key truth God taught me about myself and who I am through today's devotional?

3. What step does God want me to take in response to what He taught me in today's devotional?

DAY 9:
FREE FROM THE LAW
OF SIN AND DEATH IN CHRIST

"For the law of the Spirit of life has set you free **in Christ** Jesus from the law of sin and death."
(Romans 8:2)

The Italian Renaissance sculptor / painter Michelangelo is best-known for painting scenes from Genesis on the ceiling of the Sistine Chapel in Rome, and for his marble sculpture of David from the Bible. But when Michelangelo died, he intentionally left a series of four sculpting projects unfinished. He made four figures—the Bearded Slave, the Atlas Slave, the Awakening Slave, and the Young Slave—stuck in the very stone they were carved from. The series was called "Prisoners." Their bodies merge from the marble, muscles flexing, but they are not completely free. Michelangelo wanted to show what it might feel like to be forever enslaved.

The plight of the figures in the "Prisoners" sculpture depicts our real-life inability to pull ourselves free from the unrelenting grasp of "the law of sin and death" (Romans 8:2b). Yet, as Paul declares in Romans 8:2a: "the law of the Spirit of life has set you free in Christ Jesus from the law of sin and death." Unlike Michelangelo's unfinished "Prisoners," we're no longer bound by sin; rather, we are safe, secure, and free in Christ. Let's look at the two laws that Paul mentions in Romans 8:2, beginning with the law of sin and death.

> At salvation, a believer is freed forever from the law of sin which results in death, and is placed into a new, Spirit-governed sphere of liberty and life.

The law of sin condemns us and leads to death. The word "law" which is used twice in Romans 8:2 describes the principle by which something works. For example, the principle behind the law of gravity is that when you throw a ball into the air, gravity pulls it downward to the earth. The principle behind the "law of sin and death" (v.2b) is that sin condemns us and pulls us away from God and downward to death. We live helplessly under the law of sin and death.

The law of the Spirit frees us and leads to life. Just as the law of aerodynamics supersedes the law of gravity and frees an airplane to remain in the air, the "law of the Spirit and life" (v.2a) supersedes and abolishes the law of sin and death and leads us Godward to life. "It is the Spirit who gives life" (Jn.6:63).

A person in Christ is protected forever from the law of sin and death. Romans 8:3 declares: "For God has done what the law, weakened by the flesh, could not do. By sending his own Son in the likeness of sinful flesh and for sin, he condemned sin in the flesh." Jesus came as a man and paid sin's penalty of death for us. The law of sin and death can never again have claim over the believer in Christ. We now live in a new sphere governed by the law of the Spirit of life! "If the Son sets you free, you will be free indeed" (Jn.8:36).

Michelangelo's "Prisoners" sculpture was not the only sculpture he did that featured four figures. At age 73, he sculpted a new statue for his own grave. This sculpture, known as Florentine Pietà, included four people, all carved from the same block of marble. One of the figures is Nicodemus, whose appearance strongly resembles portraits other artists made of Michelangelo. Art critics agree that it was intended by Michelangelo to be a self-portrait. He apparently saw in himself a man who, like Nicodemus, was fearful at first to show his faith in Christ, but later stood by his faith. The other three figures depict Christ, just removed from the cross, and Mary Magdalene and Jesus' mother Mary, embracing the body of Jesus as Nicodemus looked on compassionately. This was Michelangelo's last sculpture—a personal testimony of faith.

In his "Prisoners" sculpture, Michelangelo demonstrated that he understood that "the law of sin and death" has an authority and power over us that that leads to enslavement and death. But in his "Florentine Pietà" sculpture, he also expressed the "law of the Spirit and life" that sets us free in Christ Jesus.

"In Christ" Prayer of Gratitude:
Thank You, Lord, that the law of the Spirit and life in Christ has set me free from the law of sin and death.

For Further Bible Study: How do Proverbs 4:15, 1 Peter 5:8-9, and Ephesians 6:17 address the topics of overcoming temptations and sin?

Questions to Dig Deeper

1. What is a key truth God taught me about Himself and His character through today's devotional?

   _____
   _____
   _____
   _____
   _____
   _____
   _____
   _____

2. What is a key truth God taught me about myself and who I am through today's devotional?

   _____
   _____
   _____
   _____
   _____
   _____
   _____
   _____

3. What step does God want me to take in response to what He taught me in today's devotional?

   _____
   _____
   _____
   _____
   _____
   _____
   _____
   _____

DAY 10: SEALED WITH THE HOLY SPIRIT IN CHRIST

"**In him**, you…were sealed with the promised Holy Spirit." (Ephesians 1:13)

In the World War II Battle of Savo Island in August of 1942, the USS Astoria, a U.S. Navy battle cruiser, faced off against the Japanese cruiser Chokai. The Astoria took many damaging hits and began to sink. The gun turret that 3rd Class Signalman Elgin Staples was manning exploded, sweeping him overboard. The semiconscious Staples had been hit by shrapnel in both legs and would have drowned had he not activated the tiny lifebelt around his waist at the last moment. Staples was kept afloat and alive by the lifebelt. Staples and 500 other battle survivors were rescued by the USS President Jackson a few hours later. On board the transport, Staples, hugging his lifebelt gratefully, gave it a thorough inspection for the first time. He noticed that it had been manufactured by the Firestone Tire and Rubber Company of Akron, Ohio, and had a registration number.

At home on leave, Staples described for his mother—a product inspector at Firestone—about his near-death experience and how the lifebelt manufactured at Firestone had saved his life. When Staples quoted the lifebelt's registration number, an astonished look fell over his mother's face. She said, "Every inspector at Firestone was required to affix their personal code to each item they were in charge of approving. The registration number on your lifebelt was my personal inspector's code."[7]

> The Holy Spirit performs the functions of Jesus in us, including keeping us eternally secure in Him.

We who are in Christ can rest assured that we are eternally secure in salvation because our heavenly Father has affixed His "registration number" on us—He has "put his seal on us and given us his Spirit" (2 Cor.1:22). The seal of the Holy Spirit is mentioned three times in the New Testament. Let's inspect each occurrence and discover the eternal protection the seal provides for those in Christ.

43

The seal of the Holy Spirit indicates ownership. To help us understand how the seal of the Holy Spirit indicates God's ownership of us, think of a rancher who brands his cattle or marks them with an ear tag to indicate which cattle belongs exclusively and entirely to him. "God has "put his seal on us and given us the Holy Spirit" (2 Cor.1:22) to indicate that we belong exclusively and entirely to Him. This sealing of the Holy Spirit upon us occurs at the moment of salvation. Ephesians 1:13 says, "In him you also, when you heard the word of truth, the gospel of your salvation, and believed in him, were sealed with the promised Holy Spirit." Note that Paul says we were sealed with the Holy Spirit when we believed in Christ (v.13), not sometime after salvation.

The seal of the Holy Spirit indicates authenticity. Just as a notary uses a seal to guarantee the authenticity of a signature on a document, the Holy Spirit enters the believer's life as God's "legal signature" indicating the person as an authentic believer. Romans 8:9 says, "Anyone who does not have the Spirit of Christ does not belong to him." The fact that God "has put his seal on us and given us the Holy Spirit" (2 Cor.1:22) proves that we are genuine followers of Christ. The Bible knows of no Christians who do not have the Holy Spirit dwelling in them. Paul reminds the Corinthian Christians, "Do you not know that you are God's temple and that God's Spirit dwells in you?" (1 Cor.3:16). He also reminds Timothy of "the Holy Spirit who dwells within us" (2 Tim.1:14).

The seal of the Holy Spirit indicates protection. Like a king's ring signet dipped in wax and stamped on a document protected a document in the ancient world, Ephesians 4:30 says: "Do not grieve the Holy Spirit of God, by whom you were sealed for the day of redemption." Though we can bring grief to the Spirit with our sin, we can never lose the Holy Spirit—His seal upon us and indwelling of us is eternal. We have been sealed, protected, and preserved until "the day of redemption" (v.30)—the day we see Christ.

"In Christ" Prayer of Gratitude:
God, thank You that in Christ I'm sealed with the Holy Spirit, forever safe in You.

For Further Bible Study: What other ministries of the Holy Spirit in the life of a believer are highlighted in John 14:16; 16:7-15?

Questions to Dig Deeper

1. What is a key truth God taught me about Himself and His character through today's devotional?

   _____
   _____
   _____
   _____
   _____
   _____
   _____
   _____

2. What is a key truth God taught me about myself and who I am through today's devotional?

   _____
   _____
   _____
   _____
   _____
   _____
   _____
   _____

3. What step does God want me to take in response to what He taught me in today's devotional?

   _____
   _____
   _____
   _____
   _____
   _____
   _____
   _____

DAY 11:
SPIRITUALLY ROOTED AND BUILT UP IN CHRIST

"[You are] rooted and built up **in him** and established in the faith..."
(Colossians 2:7)

Bruce Barnbaum is one of the most prolific photographers of nature in the world. Specializing in traditional black and white darkroom printers, Barnbaum's work appears in galleries and museums worldwide. His book *The Art of Photography: A Personal Approach to Artistic Expression* is considered the authoritative tome on photographic insight, ideas, and instruction.

One of Barnbaum's most iconic photos is of sequoia trees, taken as he walked the Giant Forest loop trail in Sequoia National Park on the western slopes of California's Sierra Nevada mountains on a foggy September morning. Barnbaum aligned his tripod and camera at the perfect angle, and snapped his now-famous photograph, capturing the tones and textures of a sequoia wedged between the base of two cinnamon-colored, standing sequoias, with another sequoia lying on it horizontally.

> A believer is firmly rooted in Christ, enriched to grow spiritually, and permanently approved by God.

The sequoia is an uncommon and unique tree that lives under the protection of state and national forests and parks. It is the largest species of tree in the world. Consider these facts:
- Sequoias grow to 300 feet tall.
- Sequoias grow to over 100 feet in circumference at its base.
- Sequoias can weigh up to 6,000 tons.
- Sequoias can live for up to 4,000 years.

Perhaps the most fascinating aspect of sequoias is their root system. Below ground level, the roots of sequoias twist, entangle, and knot together as far as 14 feet into the earth, and can spread over an acre. Along with anchoring the sequoias, thus accounting for the tree's soaring height, hulking girth, and astonishing weight, the root system absorbs water, stores nutrients, and reproduces vegetation.[8]

To help us understand and appreciate our security in Christ, the Apostle Paul borrows from the worlds of agriculture, architecture, and the law in Colossians 2:6-7: "Therefore, as you received Christ Jesus the Lord, so walk in him, 7 rooted and built up in him and established in the faith…" Let's consider each of these images.

In Christ, we are like a tree permanently "rooted in him" (v.7a). We can look to the roots of the great sequoia trees as an illustration of the spiritual stability, security, and health we have in Christ. The word "rooted" (v.7a) speaks of being firmly fixed and permanently grounded in Christ. Note that it is something God has done for us—not something we do for ourselves—and it also indicates past action with continuing effect, meaning that we have been rooted and will always continue to be rooted in Christ since nothing can separate us from Him!

In Christ, we are like a building continuously rising, "built up in him" (v.7b). Because we are permanently rooted in Christ, we are now able to be built up in Christ like a building continuously rising. The phrase "built up" (v.7b) indicates that it is currently and continually being built up. As we cooperate with the Lord's work in us, we grow and rise toward spiritual maturity. In Philippians 1:6, Paul declares, "I am sure of this, that he who began a good work in you will bring it to completion at the day of Jesus Christ."

In Christ, we are "established in the faith" (v.7c) like a law forever ratified. The word "established" (v.7c) is a word that was used when a law was firmly decided upon and approved. Not only are we like a tree rooted firmly and permanently in Christ, and a building rising continuously, but we are also approved by God—it has been decided by Him that we are saved and eternally established. Note that the emphasis in all three-word pictures in v.7 is on what God does in and for us, not on anything we've done for God.

"In Christ" Prayer of Gratitude:
God, thank You for establishing me in Christ, building me up in Him, and forever approving me in Him.

For Further Bible Study: How do these verses highlight the believer's eternal security in Christ: John 3:15-16; 10:28-29; Romans 8:37-39?

Questions to Dig Deeper

1. What is a key truth God taught me about Himself and His character through today's devotional?

   _____
   _____
   _____
   _____
   _____
   _____
   _____
   _____

2. What is a key truth God taught me about myself and who I am through today's devotional?

   _____
   _____
   _____
   _____
   _____
   _____
   _____
   _____

3. What step does God want me to take in response to what He taught me in today's devotional?

   _____
   _____
   _____
   _____
   _____
   _____
   _____
   _____

DAY 12:
ETERNAL LIFE IN CHRIST

> "For the wages of sin is death, but the free gift of God is eternal life **in Christ** Jesus our Lord."
> (Romans 6:23)

Some cities across the great landscape of the United States have unusual names. For example, the island-city Unalaska, Alaska is not named for its inhabitants' desire to secede from the 49th state; rather, it is a shortened version of the Native Aleut word, *Agunalaksh*, used by the Unangan people who inhabit it. Ketchuptown, South Carolina is not named for the hamburger-topper. Its name comes from the fact that it was the locale of the small store where farmers would gather to "catch up" on the news. Then there's Uncertain, Texas. When the town was forming, its first citizens wrote "uncertain" on documents asking for the name of their town because they had not yet made up their minds. The name stuck! According to a recent census, the population of Uncertain, Texas is 90.[9]

But I think there are more people—Christians in particular—who reside in "Uncertain," spiritually speaking. Our enemy, Satan, attacks the area of a Christian's assurance of salvation perhaps more than any other area. If the devil can keep us doubting our salvation, then he doesn't have to worry about us enjoying our relationship with the Lord or sharing our faith with others. Tragically, many Christians, if asked if they are saved, would write "uncertain" on the blank.

However, God does not want believers to have one ounce of uncertainty about their eternal security. The greatest blessing after being saved is knowing that you are saved and will never lose your salvation. The terms "eternal life" and "everlasting life" appear dozens of times in the New Testament in the context of assuring believers that we have it. God has gone to great lengths to assure us that when we are in Christ, we are guaranteed eternal life. Romans 6:23 is one of the clearest verses about eternal life in Christ.

> The greatest blessing after being saved is knowing that you are saved and will never lose your salvation.

Sin results in death. Romans 6:23a says, "The wages of sin is death." In the Bible, "death" refers to physical death, which is the separation of the soul from the body, and spiritual death, which is the final and eternal separation of the soul from God in hell—also called "the second death, the lake of fire" (Rev.20:14).

Those who accept Christ receive God's gift of eternal life. Romans 6:23b says, "but the free gift of God is eternal life." Although we each will experience physical death (unless Christ returns first), receiving God's gift of eternal life in Christ assures us that we will never experience the second death—final, eternal separation from God in hell (Rev.20:14).

In fact, physical death ushers the believer into an endless experience of joy, peace, and fulfillment. Paul wrote in Philippians 1:21, "For to me to live is Christ, and to die is gain." Paul understood that Christ makes life worth living today, and at death, life becomes even better because it results in more of Christ! Every believer in Christ is in the same "win-win" situation that Paul described: abundant life today in Christ (Jn.10:10) and eternal life with Christ at death (Jn.3:16)! Our eternal God cannot give eternal life temporarily.

Eternal life does not just begin in the future; it is a present reality for the believer. Romans 6:23c says, "The free gift of God is eternal life." It does not say the free gift of God will be eternal life, but that it is eternal life—present tense. John 3:36 says, "Whoever believes in the Son has [present tense!] eternal life."

Eternal life is guaranteed only through Jesus Christ. Romans 6:23d speaks of "eternal life in Christ Jesus our Lord." Because of Jesus' resurrection from the dead, He alone is qualified and capable of providing eternal life after death for all who believe in Him. 1 Corinthians 15:20-22 assures us: "Christ has been raised from the dead, the firstfruits of those who have fallen asleep. 21 For as by a man came death, by a man has come also the resurrection of the dead. 22 For as in Adam all die, so also in Christ shall all be made alive."

"In Christ" Prayer of Gratitude:
Thank You, Lord, for guaranteeing me eternal life in Christ—help me to live in certainty and assurance.

For Further Bible Study: How do John 3:16; 11:25, and 1 John 5:11-12 highlight eternal life?

Questions to Dig Deeper

1. What is a key truth God taught me about Himself and His character through today's devotional?

   _____
   _____
   _____
   _____
   _____
   _____
   _____
   _____

2. What is a key truth God taught me about myself and who I am through today's devotional?

   _____
   _____
   _____
   _____
   _____
   _____
   _____
   _____

3. What step does God want me to take in response to what He taught me in today's devotional?

   _____
   _____
   _____
   _____
   _____
   _____
   _____
   _____

DAY 13:
A PROTECTED HEART AND MIND IN CHRIST

> "And the peace of God, which surpasses all understanding, will guard your hearts and your minds **in Christ** Jesus."
> (Philippians 4:7)

William Carey (1761-1834) is known as the "father of modern missions." Carey was a pioneer missionary to India. After he was well established in his ministry in India, his supporters in England sent a printing press to assist him. Carey had spent many years learning the language so that he could produce the Scriptures in the local dialect. He had also prepared dictionaries and grammar books for the use of his successors. Thanks to the printing press, Carey was able to turn out numerous portions of the Bible for distribution.

One day while Carey was away, a fire broke out and destroyed the building, the printing press, many Bibles, and the precious manuscripts, dictionaries, and grammar books he had labored to create. When he returned and was told of the tragic loss, rather than showing despair or impatience, Carey demonstrated a remarkable peace. He knelt and thanked God that he still had the strength to do the work over again. He started immediately, not wasting a moment in self-pity or anxiety.

In England, the news of the ruin of the facilities and products—and Carey's faith-filled reaction to it—sparked an interest that sent more money and materials than he had ever received! Before his death, William Carey had duplicated and even improved on all his earlier production.[10]

> Our heart and mind are secure in Christ, forever protected by the peace of God.

The word "peace" appears dozens of times in the Bible. In reference to the peace the believer has in Christ, it does not describe an absence of turmoil, stress, or chaos. Rather, the peace of God describes a state of freedom from anxiety combined with inner contentment and confidence in God's sufficiency even in the midst of life's troubling and even devastating circumstances.

The source of peace is God. Paul refers to this quality of peace as coming from God: "the peace of God" (v.7a). God is called "the God of peace" several times in Scripture. As such, He alone can provide the genuine, lasting peace that each of us need.

Jesus drew a sharp contrast between the unique peace that He, as the Son of God, provides and the false peace the unbelieving world offers: "Peace I leave with you; my peace I give to you. Not as the world gives do I give to you. Let not your hearts be troubled, neither let them be afraid" (Jn.14:27). Paul says this peace of God "surpasses all understanding" (v.7b).

The strength of peace is supernatural. Paul says this peace of God "surpasses all understanding" (v.7b). This does not mean that the peace of God doesn't make sense; rather, it means the peace of God has a supernatural element to it since it originates with God. The peace of God is intended to be deeply, personally experienced, not merely intellectually comprehended.

The sentry of peace protects our heart and mind. Paul says the peace of God "will guard your hearts and your minds in Christ Jesus" (v.7c). Like a guard marching alertly and protectively back and forth in front of our heart and mind, the peace of God prevents fearful emotions from entering our heart and anxious thoughts from entering our mind.

The secret of peace is prayer. Philippians 4:7 indicates that the peace of God goes on "sentry duty" when we choose not to "be anxious about anything, but in everything by prayer and supplication with thanksgiving let your requests be made known to God." Refusing to worry, and instead bringing every need and request to God in prayer results in experiencing the wonderful, unique peace of God in Christ. Isaiah 26:3 says, "You keep him in perfect peace whose mind is stayed on you, because he trusts in you." According to this verse, the amount of peace we experience from God is directly proportional to how much we keep our mind focused on Him and how much we entrust control of our lives to Him.

"In Christ" Prayer of Gratitude:
Thank You, Lord, for protecting my heart and mind in Christ.

For Further Bible Study: How do Romans 15:13, 33; Philippians 4:9, and Hebrews 13:20 associate God with peace?

Questions to Dig Deeper

1. What is a key truth God taught me about Himself and His character through today's devotional?

2. What is a key truth God taught me about myself and who I am through today's devotional?

3. What step does God want me to take in response to what He taught me in today's devotional?

DAY 14:
SAFE IN GOD'S LOVE IN CHRIST

"For I am sure that neither death nor life, nor angels nor rulers, nor things present nor things to come, nor powers, 39 nor height nor depth, nor anything else in all creation, will be able to separate us from the love of God **in Christ** Jesus our Lord."
(Romans 8:38-39)

During the initial stages of the building of San Francisco's Golden Gate Bridge, construction progress was slow, almost completely stopping at times. Laborers didn't feel secure as they worked on the bridge. They couldn't concentrate on their tasks because they feared falling off the bridge. No safety devices were used, and 23 men fell to their deaths in the water 225 feet below. Engineers quickly designed and installed a massive safety net to hang underneath the bridge. After the net was in place, at least 10 men fell into it and were saved from death. Because the workers now felt secure, they could wholeheartedly serve the project, and 25% more work was accomplished each day.[11]

The workers on the bridge remind us of Christians who live in paralyzing fear that they'll lose their salvation. They can't concentrate on serving God because they're afraid they'll fall out of God's love. In Romans 8:38-39, Paul asserts that once we're saved, we're also eternally secure in God's love. Nothing will ever be able to separate us from the love of God—we are saved and loved by God eternally and forever! Once we know we're saved and secure in God's love, we can focus on the service He calls us to. Let's consider several aspects of God's unique love that assure us that we are eternally safe in His love and are in no danger of losing or falling out of His love.

> Because love is God's essential nature and quality, it guides all His intentions and activities toward us.

God's love is an indestructible love. In Romans 8:38-39, Paul lists virtually every realm and category we might think of that could threaten God's love for us. He begins with aspects of natural life: "death" (v.38a), which only brings us into Christ's glorious presence (2 Cor.5:8), and "life" (v.38b), which is full and abundant in Christ (Jn.10:10). Then Paul mentions aspects of supernatural life: "angels nor rulers [angelic powers]" (v.38c). Then he includes today and eternity: "nor things present nor things to come" (v.38c), then earthly authorities such as kings, and spiritual authorities such as Satan and demonic forces: "nor powers" (v.38d). Then he adds heaven and hell: "nor height nor depth" (v.39a)! Nothing in the natural or supernatural realms, "nor anything else in all creation" (v.39b) will be able to sever or separate us from God's love for us in Christ!

God's love is an innate love. God loves us not because of who we are, but because of who He is! 1 John 4:8 states, "God is love." Love isn't merely something God does, as if He could change His mind and not love us anymore; rather, love is something God is in His nature. God's love for us is conditioned on His own nature, not on our performance or perfection (or lack thereof!).

God's love is an immutable love. The word "immutable" means "unchanging." God declares in Malachi 3:6 that He is immutable: "I the Lord do not change." God's unchanging nature causes Him to remain eternally constant in His love for us! His love cannot increase or decrease—He loves us as much right now as He could ever possibly love us. There is nothing we could do to cause God to love us more or to love us less!

God's love is an initiating love. It was love that caused God to reach out to us amid our rebellion against Him (Rom.5:8). Any love we have for God is simply a response to the great love He initiated toward us: "We love because he first loved us" (1 Jn.4:19). Since God's love is rooted in His unchanging character and based upon His own initiative, nothing can separate us from His love.

God's love is an inexhaustible love. Paul's prayer for the Ephesians was that they would know "the love of Christ that surpasses knowledge" (Eph.3:19). This means that no matter how much of God's love we experience, there will always be more for us to experience—His love is infinite and inexhaustible!

"In Christ" Prayer of Gratitude:
Thank You, God, that in Christ I am forever secure in Your love.

For Further Bible Study: To appreciate the love of God in Christ, read 1 Corinthians 13:1-7 and substitute the name "Jesus" where it says "love."

Questions to Dig Deeper

1. What is a key truth God taught me about Himself and His character through today's devotional?

2. What is a key truth God taught me about myself and who I am through today's devotional?

3. What step does God want me to take in response to what He taught me in today's devotional?

PART 3:
YOUR SIGNIFICANCE IN CHRIST

DAY 15:
A CHILD OF GOD IN CHRIST

"**In Christ** Jesus you are all sons of God, through faith."
(Galatians 3:26)

Christian recording artist Steven Curtis Chapman has been recognized as one of the most awarded artists in the history of Christian music. He has received 59 Dove Awards, five Grammys, and has recorded more than 25 albums with 49 No.1 hits. He and his wife, Mary Beth, founded "Show Hope" which exists "to care for orphans by engaging the Church and reducing barriers to adoption."[12] In addition to their own three biological daughters, the Chapmans have three adopted daughters from China (one was tragically killed in an accident in 2008).

Steven, who calls adoption "visible gospel," said, "Until we adopted Shenandoah, I didn't fully understand the depth of what Jesus has done for us. Without Christ I was hopeless, without a future, without a name. Then Jesus came into my life, gave me hope and a future. He gave me a new name."[13]

The New Testament teaches that upon receiving Christ by faith, God adopts the believer into His family and gives His child full rights and privileges as His heirs. The Apostle John wrote, "See what kind of love the Father has given to us, that we should be called children of God; and so we are" (1 Jn.3:1).

> At salvation, God adopts us into His family as His children to experience His love, care, and provision forever.

In the Old Testament, God is presented as Father of Israel, but primarily in a corporate sense—He is the Father of the nation. But when Jesus came to earth, He introduced a new dimension to the fatherhood of God: Jesus taught and demonstrated that God is a loving and intimate Father with whom we can enjoy a personal relationship.

Of all the names for God in the Bible, particularly in the New Testament, God seems to enjoy being called "Father" the most, perhaps because "Father" so clearly indicates His love for His children.

We can learn three great truths from Romans 8:15-17 about the blessing of being a child of God in Christ.

A child of God has a new relationship with the heavenly Father. In Christ, we relate to God not as a lowly slave to an impersonal taskmaster, but as an adored child to a loving Father. "For you did not receive the spirit of slavery to fall back into fear, but you have received the Spirit of adoption as sons, by whom we cry, 'Abba! Father!'" (v.15) Note the strong contrast between the "spirit of slavery" and the "Spirit of adoption as sons" in verse v.15. Slaves were often treated harshly by their masters and lived in terror, but we are assured that we do not need to "fall back into fear" (v.15)—our heavenly Father is kind and compassionate. A slave acts out of compulsion, but a son acts out of love; a slave is moved by fear of punishment, but a son is motivated by his relationship with the father. Paul describes the unique relationship we have with God with an intimate term in v.15: "Abba" is an Aramaic word for father, similar to our English terms Daddy, or Papa. Wrapped up in "Abba" is a child's loving expression of affection and trust in his father.

A child of God has assurance of his relationship with God. "The Spirit himself bears witness with our spirit that we are children of God" (v.16). One of the surest signs that we belong to God is the presence of the Holy Spirit in our lives. The Holy Spirit enters our life at salvation to dwell within us forever (Eph.1:13). A ministry of the Holy Spirit in our life is to assure us again and again in our spirit—the deepest part of our soul—that we are His forever and He'll never leave or forsake us (Heb.13:5).

A child of God is an heir of God and fellow heir of Christ. "And if children, then heirs of God and fellow heirs with Christ" (v.17). Since we are God's children, we are also God's beneficiaries. We have an eternal inheritance awaiting us in heaven. Peter says it is "an inheritance that is imperishable, undefiled, and unfading, kept in heaven for you" (1 Pet.1:4).

"In Christ" Prayer of Gratitude:
Lord, thank You for adopting me into Your forever family in Christ, and being my loving Abba and caring Father.

For Further Bible Study: How do these verses highlight the characteristics of our loving heavenly Father: Psalm 68:5, Isaiah 64:8, Matthew 23:9, John 4:23-24; 10:30?

Questions to Dig Deeper

1. What is a key truth God taught me about Himself and His character through today's devotional?

2. What is a key truth God taught me about myself and who I am through today's devotional?

3. What step does God want me to take in response to what He taught me in today's devotional?

DAY 16:
A NEW CREATION IN CHRIST

> "If anyone is **in Christ**, he is a new creation.
> The old has passed away; behold, the new has come."
> (2 Corinthians 5:17)

In his book *A Song of Ascents*, E. Stanley Jones (1884-1973), who Time Magazine called in 1938 "the world's greatest missionary," tells about a man in Africa who, after receiving Christ, changed his name to "After." The man explained that he did so because everything significant in his life happened after he met Christ![14]

All of us who know Christ as the Forgiver of our sins and Leader of our lives can agree with "After"—everything important in our lives happened after we received Christ. When we are in Christ, we become something new—something we have never been before. Our significance is rooted in the righteousness of Christ which has been credited to us. No longer are we chained to the identity of our sinful, fallen selves. In the verses surrounding 2 Corinthians 5:17, which calls each of us "a new creation in Christ," we learn that new perspectives on several key aspects of life accompany our transformation in Christ.

As new creations in Christ, we have a new perspective on death. 2 Corinthians 5:1 says, "For we know that if the tent that is our earthly home is destroyed, we have a building from God, a house not made with hands, eternal in the heavens. 2 For in this tent we groan, longing to put on our heavenly dwelling." Paul describes our current body, or "home"

> By God's grace, we are transformed and empowered to live significant lives in delightful, vibrant union with Christ!

(v.1), as a tent. A tent is not a permanent structure—it is put up quickly and taken down quickly. Similarly, we will not live in this body forever: "It is appointed for man to die once, and after that comes judgment" (Heb.9:27), and our time in this present body is brief: "For you are a mist that appears for a little time and then vanishes" (Jms.4:14). True, our current body is weak, sinful, and dying, and we "groan" (v.2) with longing for "our heavenly dwelling" (v.2). God has an after-death plan for all who are in Christ that involves no sighing, no crying, and no dying (Rev.21:4)! We see death differently now!

As new creations in Christ, we have a new perspective on life. 2 Corinthians 5:9 says, "So whether we are at home or away, we make it our aim to please him." We no longer see our life's purpose as being to please ourselves. Now that we are new creations in Christ, we recognize our life's purpose as being to please God. The New Testament specifies several ways to please the Lord. For example, when we have faith, we please God since "without faith it is impossible to please him" (Heb.11:6). When we share the Gospel with nonbelievers, we please God: "Just as we have been approved by God to be entrusted with the gospel, so we speak, not to please man, but to please God" (1 Thess.2:4). When we do good and generously share what we have, "such sacrifices are pleasing to God" (Heb.13:16). Our life's aim now is to "do what pleases him" (1 Jn.3:22).

As new creations in Christ, we have a new perspective on Christ. 2 Corinthians 5:16 says, "Even though we once regarded Christ according to the flesh, we regard him thus no longer." We no longer look at Christ as we did in our fallen condition. Now we regard Christ in truth, understanding Him as He presents Himself in God's Word and in our personal relationship with Him. With deep conviction and joy, we believe and declare that Jesus is God (Jn.1:1, 14), our Savior (2 Pet.1:1) the eternal Alpha and Omega (Rev.1:8), and the King of kings and Lord of lords (Rev.19:16)!

As new creations in Christ, we have a new perspective on others. 2 Corinthians 5:20 says that "we are ambassadors for Christ, God making his appeal through us." We understand that apart from Christ, people are "dead in their trespasses and sins" and "without hope and without God in the world" (Eph.2:1, 12). As Christ's loyal and loving ambassadors, we represent Christ and His kingdom, and we communicate His message with the aim that all be reconciled to Him in Christ just as we have been.

"In Christ" Prayer of Gratitude:
Thank You, Lord, for making me into a new creation in Christ.

For Further Bible Study: What do Romans 6:6-7 and Ephesians 4:24 teach about our new life in Christ?

Questions to Dig Deeper

1. What is a key truth God taught me about Himself and His character through today's devotional?

   _____
   _____
   _____
   _____
   _____
   _____
   _____
   _____

2. What is a key truth God taught me about myself and who I am through today's devotional?

   _____
   _____
   _____
   _____
   _____
   _____
   _____
   _____

3. What step does God want me to take in response to what He taught me in today's devotional?

   _____
   _____
   _____
   _____
   _____
   _____
   _____
   _____

DAY 17:
CREATED FOR GOOD WORKS IN CHRIST

"We are his workmanship, created **in Christ** Jesus for good works, which God prepared beforehand, that we should walk in them." (Ephesians 2:10)

Malcolm Muggeridge was a British journalist, author, and media personality. During World War II, he worked for the British government as a soldier and a spy. Muggeridge was also a declared atheist. At the age of 79 he was converted to Christ. When asked to explain his remarkable conversion, Muggeridge said he could resist all the great books and all the great sermons about Christianity. However, he could not resist the influence of a living faith evidenced by good works for God's glory. This living faith was demonstrated in Mother Teresa who ministered to the poor in Calcutta, India in the name of Christ. When Muggeridge saw her life, he concluded, "If this is faith, I've got to have it. Hers is a light that can never be extinguished." Muggeridge went on to write the books *Jesus, the Man Who Lives*; *Christ and the Media*; and the book that introduced Mother Teresa to the Western World: *Something Beautiful for God*.[15]

Part of our significance as human beings created in the image of God (Gen.1:26-27) is found in our call to work for Him. Our life in Christ not only involves being saved from something, but also being saved for something—to do good works for Him. Let's note several truths from today's key verse, Ephesians 2:10.

We belong to God. We are "his" workmanship (v.10a). As our Creator and Savior, God has rightful claim over us! The fact that we are God's possession is reflected in 1 Corinthians 6:19, "Your body is a temple of the Holy Spirit ...You are not your own," and Titus 2:14: "who gave himself for us to purify for himself a people for his own possession." We willingly and happily yield ourselves to His loving and caring ownership and His will for our lives.

> God wants to display Himself through the good works He has preordained for us to do every day.

We are God's individual, unique works of art who exhibit His creativity and fulfill His purposes. The word "workmanship" (v.10) comes from the Greek word *poiema*, from which we also get our English word poem. Just as a poem shows the poet's originality and purpose, our unique God-given strengths and talents express God's creativity and the purposes He wants us to fulfill. Our significance is found in fulfilling God's plans for our lives.

God has tailor-made certain good works for each of us to walk in and do. "God prepared [the good works He wants us to do] beforehand, that we should walk in them" (v.10). It is astonishing to realize that God created us, and then re-created us in Christ, to accomplish specific purposes in accordance with His preordained plan for each of us. The good works God has preordained for each of us to do will almost always be in line with the unique strengths, talents, and gifts He has given each of us.

A story (likely a legend) is told about the renowned French artist Paul Gustave Dore (1832-1883). He was traveling in Europe when he ran into a dilemma at a border crossing. He had lost his passport, and despite his efforts to convince the customs officer of his identity, the officer would not allow him to pass without his proper documentation. The customs officer called his supervisor to help solve the predicament. The supervisor had never met Dore or seen Dore in person, but he was very familiar with Dore's unique journal illustrations—pictures Dore drew to illustrate Cervante's Don Quixote, Edgar Alen Poe's The Raven, and even a new English translation of the Bible. The supervisor decided to give Dore a test to prove his identity. Handing Dore a piece of paper and a pencil, he told Dore to draw a group of nearby people. Dore did so with ease. The supervisor, recognizing Dore's unique style, was convinced that he was indeed the famed artist and let him pass through the border. Paul Gustave Dore's identity was affirmed through his work.

Similarly, Jesus said that people can identify us as His followers through our unique good works for God: "Let your light shine before others, so that they may see your good works and give glory to your Father who is in heaven" (Mat.5:16).

"In Christ" Prayer of Gratitude:
Thanks, Lord, for good works I'm created in Christ to do for You.

For Further Bible Study: What do James 2:26 and Hebrews 13:16 say about the importance of good works?

Questions to Dig Deeper

1. What is a key truth God taught me about Himself and His character through today's devotional?

   _____
   _____
   _____
   _____
   _____
   _____
   _____
   _____

2. What is a key truth God taught me about myself and who I am through today's devotional?

   _____
   _____
   _____
   _____
   _____
   _____
   _____
   _____

3. What step does God want me to take in response to what He taught me in today's devotional?

   _____
   _____
   _____
   _____
   _____
   _____
   _____
   _____

DAY 18:
UNIFIED WITH BELIEVERS IN CHRIST

"There is neither Jew nor Greek, there is neither slave nor free, there is no male and female, for you are all one **in Christ** Jesus." (Galatians 3:28)

In his book *What if Jesus Had Never Been Born?* the late D. James Kennedy tells a dramatic story of the power of the Gospel. During World War II, Sergeant Jacob De Shazer served as a bombardier in General Doolittle's squadron. During a bombing mission over Japan, anti-aircraft fire struck De Shazar's bomber, causing him and his crew to bail out. They tried to elude the enemy but were soon captured and placed in a POW camp. The men were subjected to such horrific torment that De Shazer's only thought was to exact revenge on his torturers. However, one day a Bible was brought into the camp, and as De Shazer read about God's great love and forgiveness in Christ, the hate in his heart toward the Japanese melted. In fact, when the war ended, Jacob De Shazer returned to Japan as a Gospel missionary to the Japanese people.

A tract detailing Jacob's life and conversion to Christ was published. One of the tracts was given to a Japanese man in Tokyo who harbored deep resentment against the United States for its restrictions against Asian immigration. Profoundly impacted by what he read, the man received Christ, forgave the U.S., and became a Christian evangelist. The man's name was Captain Mitsuo

> A believer's racial, social, and economic status has no effect whatsoever on their standing in Christ or union with other believers.

Fuchida, the Japanese Imperial Navy officer who, on December 7, 1941, launched the first wave of air attacks on Pearl Harbor with the words, "Tora! Tora! Tora!" Fuchida returned to Pearl Harbor on the 25th anniversary of the attack with a gift for the survivors, a Bible with the words of Luke 23:43 inscribed: "Father, forgive them for they know not what they do."[16] By God's grace, Jacob de Shazer and Mitsuo Fuchida overcame their hatred and discovered that all believers have an equal share in the blessings of Christ and fellowship with all other believers.

While there are many things that separate us as human beings such as race, economic standing, and social status, Paul emphasizes in Galatians 3:28 that these differences have no effect on a believer's standing in the Lord or union with other believers in Christ: "There is neither Jew nor Greek, there is neither slave nor free, there is no male and female, for you are all one in Christ Jesus."

Distinctions in race have no effect on one's standing in Christ. Galatians 3:28a says, "There is neither Jew nor Greek…for you are all one in Christ." God does not show favoritism even to His chosen people, the Jews. Luke and Cornelius are examples of Gentile believers, while Matthew, Peter, and Paul are examples of Jewish believers in the New Testament—and all were united in Christ.

Distinctions in social and economic status have no effect on one's standing in Christ. Galatians 3:28b says, "There is neither…slave nor free…for you are all one in Christ." Whether a believer is a poor slave like Onesimus (Phm.1:16), or a wealthy noble like Philemon (Phm.1:2), all Christ-followers are equal in Christ.

Distinctions between male and female have no effect on one's standing in Christ. Galatians 3:28c says, "there is no male and female, for you are all one in Christ." The dozens of Christian men and women listed in the New Testament remind us that each had an equal share in Christ, as do we Christians today.

A question on the topic of Christian unity comes up: "If unity among Christians is so important, why are there so many different denominations?" The existence of different denominations in Christianity does not necessarily indicate disunity. True Christians agree on all the essentials that make Christianity what it is—there is great consensus among followers of Christ on these major matters. Disagreements between Christians are usually on nonessential issues such as how church leadership should be organized, use of spiritual gifts, denominational traditions, details of Christ's second coming, etc.—none of which affect the veracity of Christianity. Christians are committed to unity in essentials, liberty in nonessentials, and charity in all things.

"In Christ" Prayer of Gratitude:
Thank You, Lord, that in Christ I am united with all believers.

For Further Bible Study: What do Psalm 133:1, Romans 15:6, and Philippians 2:2 say about unity?

Questions to Dig Deeper

1. What is a key truth God taught me about Himself and His character through today's devotional?

2. What is a key truth God taught me about myself and who I am through today's devotional?

3. What step does God want me to take in response to what He taught me in today's devotional?

DAY 19:
A NEW WALK IN CHRIST

"Therefore, as you received Christ Jesus the Lord,
so walk **in him**."
(Colossians 2:6)

Stephen Olford, born in 1918, lived the first 17 years of his life in Angola where his parents were faithful missionaries for many years. After high school, Olford moved to England for college, where he said his heart grew cold toward God. He became obsessed with racing motorcycles—the faster the better.

One night after winning a race, Olford was going home on his motorcycle, felt the front tire wobble, crashed, and lay on the icy road for hours with a severe concussion. He was found and taken to a hospital where he developed a life-threatening case of pneumonia. With no treatment available, the doctors sent him home, giving him little chance of surviving. Olford said later that as a battle was taking place in his body an even greater battle was taking place in his heart. He knew he had strayed from God and was living to indulge his own desires.

> In Christ, we have a new walk—a transformed, Holy Spirit-empowered lifestyle expressed through God-honoring thoughts, words, and deeds.

Back in Angola, Olford's missionary father had not heard of Stephen's critical condition. There were no phones in the Angola jungle, and it took three months for a letter to get from England to Angola and another three months to get from Angola to England. Stephen often received letters from his parents with updates on the mission work. But when Stephen, dying at home, opened this letter from his father, written weeks before the motorcycle accident had happened, he read these words, "My son, this is of utmost importance: 'Only one life, will soon be past; only what's done for Christ will last.'"

His heart pierced by the words, Stephen, despite his weak condition, knelt by his bed and prayed an "all in" prayer of dedication. He also prayed for healing. Olford later said that prayer was a turning point in his life—he let go of his own way of life and gave himself fully to Christ. God granted his request. Stephen was healed, his life was spared, and he became a godly, faithful pastor.[17]

Billy Graham said Stephen Olford was "the man who most influenced my ministry."[18]

Colossians 2:6 tells us to "walk in [Christ]." The Bible uses the word "walk" to describe the way of life of a person who is in Christ. Stephen Olford's walk—his way of life—was dramatically changed by Christ. He lived his life with a focus on following Christ. Here are three other ways the Bible describes our new walk in Christ:

We walk by faith. 2 Corinthians 5:7 says, "We walk by faith, not by sight." While we feel deeply the pain, suffering, and evil of this broken world, by faith we focus on the sufficient grace, daily strength, sustaining peace, and bright hope the Lord alone provides.

We walk with transformed, renewed minds, pursuing truth. Ephesians 4:17 says, "You must no longer walk as the Gentiles [unbelievers] do, in the futility of their minds." We love God with all our mind (Mat.22:37) as we "test everything; hold fast what is good. Abstain from every form of evil" (1 Thess.5:21-22).

We walk in a Christ-honoring manner. Eph.4:1 says, "Walk in a manner worthy of the calling to which you have been called." Knowing all that Jesus did to save us, we want to live holy lives, staying as far away from sin as possible.

The story is told of a medieval king who wanted to hire someone to be his chariot driver. He chose three men who were considered to be the best drivers in the kingdom and took them to a high cliff with a sheer drop of over a thousand feet. The king told them to drive along the rugged road. The first two drivers drove as fast and as close to the edge as they could, demonstrating how well they could maneuver the chariot right on the edge. The third driver drove fast, but far away from the cliff's edge. When asked why he drove far from cliff's edge, he replied, "The person I'll be carrying is so important that I don't want to take any risks." The king chose him. Our testimony for Christ is too important for us to take risks with sin—let's stay as far away from sin as we can in our new walk.[19]

"In Christ" Prayer of Gratitude:
Thank You, Lord, for changing my life and
giving me a new walk in Christ.

For Further Bible Study: What qualities of the Christian walk are listed in Ephesians 4:1-3?

Questions to Dig Deeper

1. What is a key truth God taught me about Himself and His character through today's devotional?

   _____
   _____
   _____
   _____
   _____
   _____
   _____

2. What is a key truth God taught me about myself and who I am through today's devotional?

   _____
   _____
   _____
   _____
   _____
   _____
   _____

3. What step does God want me to take in response to what He taught me in today's devotional?

   _____
   _____
   _____
   _____
   _____
   _____
   _____

DAY 20:
ALWAYS TRIUMPHANT IN CHRIST

"Thanks be to God, who **in Christ** always leads us in triumphal procession, and through us spreads the fragrance of the knowledge of him everywhere."
(2 Corinthians 2:14)

E. M. Bartlett was born on Christmas Eve, 1883 in Waynesville, Missouri. His family later moved to Arkansas where Bartlett was trained as a music teacher and began writing and publishing Southern gospel music. In 1918, he partnered with David Moore and Will Ramsey to start the Hartford Music Institute. Through his institute, Bartlett published hymns, periodicals, and magazines, and provided opportunities for numerous gospel music songwriters and musicians to develop their skills and broaden their ministries.

> Victory in Jesus is not found in doing our best for Him, but in allowing Him to do His best in us.

A profound songwriter himself, Bartlett wrote dozens of hymns and even experienced success in the country music world. But in 1939 at age 56, tragedy struck: Bartlett suffered a paralyzing stroke that rendered him bedridden, unable to walk or even speak.

Bartlett's friends thought Bartlett's teaching and songwriting ministry was over. But it was during these dark, difficult days that Bartlett wrote his best-known hymn. He said that while confined to his bed, he began to look back over his life to the day he accepted Christ and the blessed life he had lived since then. He picked up a pen and wrote the first verse to "Victory in Jesus":

"I heard an old, old story, how a Savior came from glory;
how he gave His life on Calvary to save a wretch like me.
I heard about His groaning, of His precious blood's atoning;
then I repented of my sins and won the victory."

After this first refrain, Bartlett wrote the chorus:

"O victory in Jesus: my Savior, forever. He sought me and bought me with His redeeming blood. He loved me 'ere I

knew Him, and all my love is due Him. He plunged
me to victory beneath the cleansing flood."

Bartlett's son, Eugene, was also a gospel singer and began to travel around the country, continuing his father's music ministry. Eugene introduced "Victory in Jesus" to thousands during his travels. E.M. Bartlett died in 1941, but his hymn of triumph in Christ continues to live and inspire Christians around the world today.[20]

The idea of rejoicing and singing amid suffering is a concept unique to Christianity. Like E.M. Bartlett, we who know the Lord find in the following three resources the comfort, strength, and confidence to speak and sing of triumph in Jesus even in our darkest and most difficult days.

We are always triumphant in Christ because we have a Savior who has experienced our pain. Jesus knows how we feel when we're hurting. As a man "of sorrows and acquainted with grief" (Is.53:3), Jesus loved us enough to come to earth and enter our pain with us. Yet, because He is God, we are "more than conquerors through him who loved us" (Rom.8:37).

We are always triumphant in Christ because of His promises to redeem our suffering. Promises like Romans 8:28: "We know that for those who love God all things work together for good, for those who are called according to his purpose" assure us that we have victory in Jesus who "has overcome the world" (Jn.16:33). God turns our scars into stories of His redeeming power.

We are always triumphant in Christ because He will return one day to end all suffering and bring all evildoers to justice. Romans 21:4 says, "He will wipe away every tear from their eyes, and death shall be no more, neither shall there be mourning, nor crying, nor pain anymore, for the former things have passed away." God's promise of ultimate victory in Christ gives us hope and prompts us to rejoice and sing of our victory in Jesus today.

"In Christ" Prayer of Gratitude:
Thank You, Lord, for causing me to always triumph in Christ.

For Further Bible Study: How does 1 Corinthians 15:50-58 highlight our victory in Jesus?

Questions to Dig Deeper

1. What is a key truth God taught me about Himself and His character through today's devotional?

2. What is a key truth God taught me about myself and who I am through today's devotional?

3. What step does God want me to take in response to what He taught me in today's devotional?

DAY 21:
HOPE IN CHRIST

"Remembering before our God and Father your...steadfastness of hope **in our Lord Jesus Christ**."
(1 Thessalonians 1:3)

Bartolomeu Dias (1450-1500) is considered to be one of the greatest Portuguese explorers of the Atlantic Ocean. In 1488, he led the first European expedition around the cape at the southern tip of Africa, opening the trade route to Asia by way of the Atlantic and Indian Oceans. However, Dias almost didn't make it. Warm water currents from the east run into the cold currents from the northwest, resulting in severe weather and dangerous waves around the cape. As Dias sailed around the cape, the storms were treacherous—his ship was battered and nearly sank—he nearly didn't finish the journey. As a result of the difficulties he endured, Dias named that point of land extending into the ocean the "Cape of Storms."

Years later, Vasco da Gama (1460-1524), also a Portuguese sea explorer, sailed the same route. But, unlike Dias who focused on the danger and risk, the optimistic de Gama chose to focus on the jewels and treasures of India to which the trade route opened way. Vasco de Gama changed the name the "Cape of Storms" to the "Cape of Good Hope" and the name has remained.[21]

We all go through storms in life. But as believers in Christ, rather than dwelling on life's difficulties, we can focus on God's good purposes and power in the storm, looking ahead to the redemption awaiting us in heaven after all storms have passed. In Christ, we live lives of good hope.

> For those in Christ, hope is the steady confidence that God is in control of all things and that He will fulfill every promise He has made.

There is a big difference between a Christian's hope in Christ and what the unbelieving world calls hope. To the world, hope is simply blind optimism or wishful thinking. Their hope is put in people, technology, and human solutions, but all those can fail. In contrast, biblical hope is the confidence that the God who will not fail and "is faithful" (1 Cor.1:9) is in control of all things. He will fulfill every promise He ever made to us in Christ, and He will complete His good plan for us. Hebrews

7:19 describes our hope as "a better hope…through which we draw near to God." Indeed, our hope is not just in Christ, our hope is Christ: "Christ Jesus [is] our hope" (1 Tim.1:1). Here is a sampling of descriptive terms the Bible associates with our hope in Christ.

Ours is a confident hope that saves us. 1 Thessalonians 5:8 speaks of "the hope of salvation." This is the confidence that God will complete all that He started in us at salvation. Paul declared, "I am sure of this, that he who began a good work in you will bring it to completion at the day of Jesus Christ" (Php.1:6). Note that salvation is a "good work" (v.6)—God always does a better work for us than we can do for ourselves! Lastly, God "will bring it completion" (v.6)—He always finishes what He started. Let's rejoice that God does not give up on us when we are in Christ!

Ours is a good hope that sustains us. 2 Thessalonians 2:16 says, "May our Lord Jesus Christ…and God our Father, who loved us and gave us eternal comfort and good hope through grace, comfort your hearts and establish them in every good work and word" (2 Thess.2:16-17). Paul's prayer was for believers who were suffering persecution for their faith. He assures them that their hope was a "good hope" (v.16): it was profitable and would pay off in establishing them in their faith as they endured hardship.

Ours is a blessed hope that sanctifies us. Paul refers to our hope in Christ's return motivating us to live godly lives: "Training us to renounce ungodliness and worldly passions, and to live self-controlled, upright, and godly lives in the present age, waiting for our blessed hope, the appearing of our great God and Savior Jesus Christ" (Titus 2:12-13). Our hope in Christ's return is "blessed" (v.12)—it is a prosperous hope that enriches us as we await His return. There is, perhaps, no greater motivation for godly living than knowing Christ could return at any moment: "We know that when he appears we shall be like him…everyone who thus hopes in him purifies himself" (1 Jn.3:2-3).

"In Christ" Prayer of Gratitude:
Thank You, Lord, that in Christ my hope is stable and secure.

For Further Bible Study: What do Colossians 1:27 and 1 Peter 1:3 say about hope?

Questions to Dig Deeper

1. What is a key truth God taught me about Himself and His character through today's devotional?

   _____
   _____
   _____
   _____
   _____
   _____
   _____

2. What is a key truth God taught me about myself and who I am through today's devotional?

   _____
   _____
   _____
   _____
   _____
   _____
   _____

3. What step does God want me to take in response to what He taught me in today's devotional?

   _____
   _____
   _____
   _____
   _____
   _____
   _____

Notes

1. Sdoia, Roseann, *Perfect Strangers: Friendship, Strength, and Recovery AfterBoston's Worst Day* (New York: Public Affairs, (2017)
2. Lutzer, Erwin, *How You Can Be Sure That You Will Spend Eternity with God* (Chicago: Moody Press, 1996), 41
3. Wiersbe, Warren, *Key Words of the Christian Life: Understanding and Applying Their Meanings* (Grand Rapids: Baker Books, 2002), 19-20
4. Lutzer, *How You Can Be Sure*, 67-68
5. Gray, Alice, *More Stories for the Heart* (Sisters: Multnomah, 1997), 15
6. "Double Jeopardy." Cornell Law School. Accessed November 1, 2023. https://www.law.cornell.edu/wex/double_jeopardy
7. "A Mother's Life-Belt." The National World War II Museum. May 12, 2012. http://www.nww2m.com/2012/05/a-mothers-life-preserver
8. "Giant Sequoias." National Park Service. October 16, 2023. https://www.nps.gov/seki/learn/nature/bigtrees.htm
9. "Uncertain Texas." World Population Review. January 2023. https://worldpopulationreview.com/us-cities/uncertain-tx-pop
10. Severance, Diane. "William Carey's Amazing Mission." Christianity.com. April 28, 2010. https:// www.Christianity.com/church/church-history/timeline/1701-1800/william-careys-amazing-mission-11630319.html
11. "Golden Gate Bridge Construction." Golden Gate Bridge Highway & Transportation District. https://www.goldengate.org/bridge/history-research/bridge-construction/construction
12. "Show Hope: Our Story." Show Hope. Accessed October 4, 2023. https://showhope.org/about-us/our-story/
13. "The Story Behind Steven Adopting Three Chinese Children." Stephen Curtis Chapman: I Will Be Here. January 22, 2006. https://iwillbehere.wordpress.com/2006/01/22/the-story-behind-steven-adopting-three-chinese-children
14. Jones, E. Stanley, *A Song of Ascents* (Nashville: Abington Press, 1968), 16
15. Wolfe, Gregory, Malcolm Muggeridge: A Biography, (Grand Rapids: Eerdmans Publishing Company, 1995), 411
16. Kennedy, D. James, *What if Jesus Had Never Been Born?* (Nashville: Thomas Nelson, 1994), 196-197

[17] Willmore, Roger D., "First Person: A Tribute to Steven Olford." Baptist Press. September 3, 2004. https://www.baptistpress.com/resource-library/news/first-person-a-tribute-to-stephen-olford

[18] Phillips, John, *Only One Life: The Biography of Stephen Olford*, (Neptune: Loizeaux, 1995), 294

[19] Graham, Billy. *A Biblical Standard for Evangelists*. (Minneapolis: World Wide Publications, 1984), 76

[20] "Victory in Jesus," Hymnary. Accessed November 3, 2023. https://hymnary.org/i_heard_an_old_old_story_how_a_savior

[21] "The Cape of Good Hope," Earth Observatory. May 28, 2019. https://earthobservatory.nasa.gov/images/145476/the-cape-of-good-hope

ABOUT THE AUTHOR

Larry Starkey is a pastor and Bible teacher who loves to help people in their walk with God. He and his wife, Ethel, live in West Palm Beach, Florida.

www.ingramcontent.com/pod-product-compliance
Lightning Source LLC
Chambersburg PA
CBHW020945090426
42736CB00010B/1274